lines by livvy

Livvy Leigh

BookLeaf Publishing
India | USA | UK

Presentation by *BookLeaf Publishing*

Web: www.bookleafpub.com

E-mail: info@bookleafpub.com

ISBN: 9789357449526

First edition 2022

DEDICATION

to the people who love me, even when i have
trouble loving myself

PREFACE

"But in the end, stories are about one person saying to another: This is the way it feels to me. Can you understand what I'm saying? Does it feel this way to you?"

—Kazuo Ishiguro, in his Nobel prize (2017) acceptance speech

my first vow

i thought
for the longest time
that people must read
the words i write

tricked myself into thinking
that writing only counts
when there's someone there
to voice their doubts

the death of an author
the rise of the reader

lo and behold
the writer's block came in strong
because all the words
i brought to paper
felt incredibly wrong

i was writing about things
i didn't really know
i broke the number one rule
yet still had nothing to show

the rise of an author
the death of the reader

so i vow to myself
from now on all i'll do
is write the words
i know to be true

true in the sense
i'm not writing to be read
i'm writing because
it needs to be said

a happy beginning

give me a happy beginning
and a happy inbetween
because honestly how happy
Can an ending be?
saying goodbye is always hard
the ending is always the sad part
so i won't ask for a happy one
just give me a happy start

lost

i'm lost at sea
in this tiny little boat,
i'd tell you more but
word's get stuck in my throat,
they're there somewhere
simmering beneath my skin,
in fact,
there's so so many,
i never know where to begin

my one page on you

my fingers ache to type out words to you
nothing much, simply a line or two
just something to get me on your mind
the same way you seem to be on mine

but i hesitate, end up in my notes instead
my one page on you
full of things never sad

and maybe someday i'll show you
and then you'll see
the exact effect you've had on me

sane

i want to talk to you
but i never know what to say
because how can i be casual
about convincing you to stay

i hide behind my language
and everything i rhyme
but every word is written
with you on my mind

does that make me romantic
or just really, really sad?
either way thoughts of you
are driving me mad

so, i'll just stop thinking
start writing you out of my brain
and maybe in doing so
i'll manage to stay sane

asking for a friend

am i still a writer
if i'm terrified of words?
can i be a feather
if i'm not that fond of birds?

am i still a singer
if i no longer have a voice?
can i be a vote
if i never make a choice?

am i still an artist
if i lost my only pen?
if the answer's always no
who am i then?

from the diary of an astronaut

the courtyard is full of life
and it seems i am in space
for there are an endless
amount of galaxies
behind each single face

universes upon universes
i will never fully grasp
an endless stream of
shooting stars
i stare until they pass

amidst all this
there is little lonely me
in my silly little space suit
floating aimlessly
not a part
but not apart
for i too am a galaxy
but there's no one paying any mind

to
little
lonely
me

my mind is an ocean

my mind is an ocean
it's endless to me
jump in a boat and
swim out to sea

see if you'll find me
i'm one with the waves
maybe you might be the one
the one who saves

i'm in danger of drowning
i'm drifting away
so come on and find me
find me a reason to stay

to family and friends,

of course,
it's not ok.

the world's a burning mess.

but with you in it,
it hurts a little less.

the dark side of the moon

loving the good parts is easy
it's learning to ride a bike
what i have not mastered yet
is loving the parts i don't like

loving the ugly and the bad,
the parts that drive me mad

loving it all is a climb
loving it all takes time

teufelskreis

there's so much and so many
i have it all, i haven't any
whirring and whizzing and
bubbling and fizzing—

can you feel it too?
i'm scared of me
i'm scared of you
retreat to the trenches
run back to the benches
take cover and hide
he's about to blow
we know how it plays out
exactly how it'll go

in the dark and in tears
is that not how it ends?
the night will be long
the morning brings amends

even if it does,
it never feels like peace
a well-oiled machine
add some extra grease
he's working once more
reset to how it was before

it is as it's always been
nothing new to be seen
drop the paper and the pen.
we're starting over again.

from a page of my little book

make art out of darkness
write to let in light
take that numbness
make it a delight

pick up a pen
let your pain be the ink
draw it out on paper
no need to think

yet the page is too blank
words perpetually scribbled out
the pen is too heavy
for fingers full of doubt

share that inner chaos
it unthreads along the way
it might be tomorrow
if it is not today

no need for force
the time will come

for now, just doodle
relieve it some

it needn't make sense
to you or to me
but it's out there now
for the world to see

or to never see
safe in this little book
where i promise
no one will ever look

i sat down by the water

i sat down by the water
waited for thoughts to come and go
i called out to the waves
can't they push me to and fro

i sat down by the water
watched the ducks swim by
i called out to the birds
won't they teach me to fly

i sat down by the water
let the sun shine down on me
i called out to the moon
does he also miss me

i sat down by the water
wrote what came to mind
i called out to the world
to not leave me behind

i'm scared

i'm scared of the future
of what is still to come

i'm scared i feel too much
i'm scared i'm going numb

the world is full of hate
when what we need is love

i'm scared all my empathy
will never be enough

i'm scared to read the news
i'm scared what i might see

yet i check it every day
how bad can it be

and it always is that bad
good news is hard to find

i'm so scared of the future
i'm scared to lose my mind

for mum

if i could wave a magic wand
and make everything alright
i hope you know that i would

if i could protect you from it all
from any past and future plight
i hope you know that i would

if i could keep you safe
from now 'til the end of time
i hope you know that i would

if i could somehow secure
that you'll forever be fine
i hope you know that i would

but sadly, i can't.
and i won't pretend,
it breaks my heart.

but,
if i could.

i hope you know
that i would.

a note to me

dear me,

i forgive you,
for not always opening up to the people you're
close to.

i forgive you,
for not always putting things away again like
you're supposed to.

i forgive you,
for harsh words spoken in haste.

i forgive you,
for the time you waste
making sure everyone is comfortable
making sure everyone's happy
when often you are not,
which is fine by the way,
you're only human after all

life is ups and downs.
sometimes you're up high
and sometimes you fall.

i forgive you,
for all the days spent in bed,
doing nothing but drowning out the noise in
your head.

i forgive you,
for all the things forgotten, the things you don't
say,
for all the things you keep safely locked away.

i forgive you,
for you are kind and smart and good.

i forgive you,
for everyone else surely would.

i forgive you,
for you are loved,
most of all by me.

i forgive you,
for you try your best
and that's enough for me.

black hole

this feels like a déjà vu
i've been here before
in this room, in these clothes
staring at this floor
trust me, i know my madness,
the last report said it was gone
but i guess some things get stuck in your head
like that one really good song

only this one makes my blood run cold,
keeps me frozen in place,
rooted to the spot with a friendly lying face.

so, tell me,
what do i do now?
how do i stay alive
when i'm being killed
by my own mind?

if i surround myself with people that are happy
and if i paint my bedroom walls yellow,
if i walk around like a human smiley,
do you think it'd be able to let go?
this darkness that lives inside me
to be honest i just want to know

is it scientifically possible to escape a black
hole?

i try to keep calm and just carry on,
wordlessly walking through these streets
just to make it to the end of the day
and curl up in my sheets
until the nightmares come
and rob me of my sleep,
don't know how much longer
i'll last or how long i can keep

asking, what do i do now?
how do i stay alive
when i'm being killed
by my own mind?

if i surround myself with people that are happy
and if i paint my bedroom walls yellow,
if i walk around like a human smiley,
it has to let me go.
this darkness lives inside me
i want you know

that i'll fight every single day
to stop you swallowing me whole.

for marie

sitting on the steps,
talking as the sun sets

occasional sip of wine,
forgetting the concept of time

just the dark, you and i,
let's never say goodbye.

aren't i so lucky?
to have you here with me
to fight off the lonely,
that's drowning me slowly.

growing

i'm growing
up towards the sun
like a sunflower in august

i'm growing
against all odds
like a dandelion through the cracks

i'm growing
so one day i bloom
like the flower i am

who am i and who are you

who am i and who are you?
are you old or am i new?
am i broken? am i bent?
are you bought or am i spent?
can i stay? are you going somewhere?
are you here or am i there?
can i be fixed or will i one day heal?
am i fake and are you real?

who am i and who are you?
i am me or am i you too?
are you me or are we us?
we're not them. what's the fuss?
i'm tired, you're sick, can we go?
you're my light, i'm my own shadow
don't leave me, i won't leave you
if you're going, can i come too?

who am i and who are you?
is there an A to every Q?
who are you and who am i?
can i take a look through your eye?

is that your blue and is that my green?
i'm the best thing i've ever seen.
i look like a person, i look so real.
i wonder about the sadness i feel.
is it still there? it looks to be gone.
it looks like no trouble carrying on
a head held high, don't i look like me?
interesting, i thought i'd never see

who am i and who are you?
curtain rises, that's our cue
the world's our stage, much to do
are we the many or are we the few?
standing ovation, but i can't see you

lights go out, enough for tonight
how do i get you to hold me tight?
i'm always here, always will be
without you there is no me

but really, before we go,
will i ever truly know?
who i am and who you are,
a supernova, a shooting star,
a black hole, a dark night,
a fantastic, an alright.
who am i and who are you?
who does it even matter to?

who am i and who are you?
come on, just one little clue.
can i exist just as i am?
i'm not sure i understand
i wonder if i ever will?
shall i take this little pill?
do you take those too?
will they help me if they help you?
will it ever stop? will i miss it if it does?
will i be better with an added buzz?

who am i and who are you?
have you ever lied like i do?
who am i and who are you?
will you tell me if it's true?
will you keep me safe?
will you hold me warm?
will you tell me when it's passed,
this raging storm?

who am i and who are you?
if only any of us knew.

loved

let the warmth engulf you
let it seep through your skin
let it chase away the cold
let it make a home within

this is what it feels like
you're as soft as you are rough
this is what it feels like
to be cherished, to be enough

enough and more
we are all so glad
you chose not to leave us
when all you knew was sad

remember this feeling
remember its warm glow
remember you are loved
more than you'll ever know